BULLSH

Published by Reed Independent, Melbourne, 2015
Based on the book 'Australian Yarns' by Ron Edwards, Rigby Ltd, 1974

Printed by Createspace.com, a division of Amazon.com

Available as a printed book or an ebook from Createspace.com or Amazon.com or Kindle estores, together with most major international online outlets or bookshops with online ordering facilities.

Copyright © Bill Reed 1974

'Bullsh' the play: copyright © 1978 Bill Reed and Ron Edwards
'Australian Yarns' the book: copyright © Ron Edwards 1974

'Drawn Cow' from Google Openclipart, uploader Frankes
Re-issue cover: Dilani Priyangika Ranaweera, Dart Lanka Productions, Colombo, Sri Lanka

National Library of Australia Cataloguing-in-Publication entry:
Creator: Reed, Bill
Title: Bullsh: or, That Bloody Cow / Bill Reed.
 ISBN: 9780994322746 (paperback)
Subjects: Australian wit, humour -- Drama. Australian drama.
Australia -- Social life and customs -- Drama.
Other Creators/Contributors: Edwards, Ron, 1930-2008. Australian yarn.
Dewey Number: A822.3

National Library of Australia Cataloguing-in-Publication entry:
Creator: Reed, Bill, 1939- author.
Title: Bullsh: or,That Bloody Cow / Bill Reed.
ISBN: 9780994322753 (ebook)
Subjects: Australian wit, humour -- Drama. Australian drama.
Australia -- Social life and customs -- Drama.
Other Creators/Contributors: Edwards, Ron, 1930-2008.
Australian yarn.
Dewey Number: A822.3

BULLSH

or

That Bloody Cow

a gab for the stage by

Bill Reed and Ron Edwards

Other works by Bill Reed
The Pipwink Papers\
Me, the Old Man
Stigmata
Ihe
Dogod
Crooks
Tusk
Throw her back
Are You Human?
Tasker Tusker Tasker
Awash
1001 Lankan Nights book 1
1001 Lankan Nights book 2
Water Workout (Nonfiction)

plays
Burke's Company
Truganinni
The Pecking Order
Mr Siggie Morrison with his Comb and Paper*
Jack Charles is Up and Fighting
Just Out of Your Ground
You Want It, Don't You, Billy?
I Don't Know What to Do with You!
Paddlesteamer
Cass Butcher Bunting
More Bullsh
Talking to a Mirror
Auntie and the Girl

award-winning short stories *(see title 'Passing Strange')*
Messman on the C.E. Altar
English Expression
The 200-year Old Feet
The Case Inside
Blind Freddie Among the Pickle Jars
The Old Ex-serviceman
Mahood on the Thin Beach
The Shades of You my Dandenong

Other works by Ron Edwards

Ron Edwards authored nearly 300 books as one of Australia's most versatile and creative authors and folk lorists. His output includes works in fiction, nonfiction (on such topics as leather working, the wheat industry), sketchbooks, travel guides, folk lore including ballads, music and oral traditions. The list goes on. He was a fine painter and illustrator in his own right.

He founded and was the guiding light behind North Queensland's favourite publishing house, The Rams Skull Press in Kuranda at ramskullpress.com, from where a full list of his books can be got with many still in print.

The National Library of Australia and all major public, school and private libraries contain full catalogue details on Ron's work as well.

The Rams Skull Press remains the oldest privately owned publishing house in Australia. The business has been owned and operated by the Edwards family for over fifty years. The very first books issued under the banner of the Rams Skull Press were printed by Ron Edwards in 1950 and were a short run of books on a traditionalist's screw press featuring linocuts created by Ron.

To Malcolm and to his sharp mind and black pen. Nothing he did was ever bull dozing.

The play

Bullsh

Premiered at the Playbox Theatre, Melbourne, on 7 July 1978.
Director   Malcolm Robertson
Designer   John Beckett
Cast: Athol Compton, Cliff Ellen, Brian Hannon, Frederick Parslow, John Wood

More Bullsh

Premiered at Playbox Theatre, Melbourne, November 1978.
Director   Malcolm Robertson
Designer   John Beckett
Cast: Cliff Ellen, Frederick Parslow, John Wood

The yarns

Based on the best-selling 'Australian Yarns' by Ron Edwards. First published by Rigby Ltd, 1974, and re-issued by the University of Queensland Press in 1996.

Individual actors are free to go their own ways with relating them, and reproduce them or reduce them according to their own rhythms.

ACT 1

(The time is later afternoon, early evening. The shadows will grow and the sunset will eventually deepen to evoke a sense of something passing.

The noise from inside the outback pub is rising and falling as it does throughout.

But right now, out here on the pun's verandah, there is a frozen moment. It is centred on MICK and POP... but SANDY and PRICKY, who are also sitting out there, seem to be waiting expectantly too.

MICK is literally staring at POP's ear from only a few centimetres away. He is not inspecting it or touching it; he is merely leaning forward towards it, having just shouted into it and now waiting breathlessly for an answer – as though the ear itself would answer back.

While we wait we observe that SANDY and PRICKY are sitting in their places so comfortably that they are obviously in their time-honoured spots. POP, too, is seated in what is significantly the only chair of the verandah. Its throne-like height somehow typifies not only his age but also the greater length of time that he has been coming to the pub.

As the 'frieze' extends in time, MICK's expectancy for the answer becomes palpable; he seems mesmerised by POP's ear and cannot take his eyes from it.

POP clears his throat. It is a signal for even SANDY and PRICKY to look up. But nothing further comes. MICK drags his attention away from the ear and 'leans' forehead-to-forehead with POP to stare unblinkingly into the old man's eyes. All he gets is an unblinking stare back.

After this anticlimax, SANDY and PRICKY go back to their own thoughts again.

Finally MICK can't stand it any longer. He yells at POP:)

MICK   WELL?!

(This scares the life out of the other two, but doesn't cause POP to turn an eyebrow.)

SANDY   Jesus wept!

MICK   (appeal) Give's a hand, you blokes.

PRICKY   (shrugs) He can't hear a word you're saying.

MICK   The old bugger's lying doggo.

PRICKY   Who?.

MICK   Why didn't you?

SANDY   Why didn't we what?

MICK (eyes upwards) Jeezwept. So why'd he ask me what I'm doing with the 'dozer here for then?

SANDY Wondering that meself. Weren't you, Pricky?

PRICKY Who?.

MICK (loses patience) Man'd get more sense out of...
   (indicates inside pub)
that mob in there and I can't understand a word of what the buggers are saying.
   (goes to stride off inside, but stops for:)
Tell me when Johnno lobs up, okay?

(and goes in. The screen door creaks as traditionally unoiled. It will be a sound that is a constant reminder that this pub is an old one that hasn't been touched by progress up to now.

Just as MICK disappears inside, POP comes to life with a bursting vengeance, shouts after him:)

POP Bring out 'nother three while you're at it, son.
   (to others)
Think he heard me?

SANDY Dunno, Pop.

POP (nudging SANDY with his foot as he does throughout) What?

SANDY   (shouts reply as he does throughout) Dunno!

POP   You never know if they're listening these days.

(Verandah frieze again.

POP again clears his throat. The other two again look his way and then turn back when nothing comes out.

But POP this time is actually winding himself for an absolute gush of words)

POP   You wouldn't read about what someone was just telling me, y'wouldn't. Goin' on about how they're 'dosing this place into the ground tomorrow. That so? My old Dad, he first come here when I was about ten, I reckon. Dyou think he could ever spit through a snake's bum at fifty paces! That's another story. Course, I could drink a bit more in those days. Started to taper off when I got around fifteen. Met the old girl, what happened. Responsibilities. Drove a man crazy, she did. That someone, he was saying some river or something coming right through here. How come I ain't ever seen a river wandering around here? Says they're going to turn this place into a lake or something. Stuff having a lake. If I want a lake I go to the dunny, don't I?
   (thinks seriously about that)
Who was saying this is the last day for this place? Says there's a big mob of high-up poofs grogging on inside on account of the place won't be standing tomorrow. Poofs! What's the flaming world coming to if a bloke can't get near his own bar for high-up poofs up from the city? You listening? If you two blokes listened instead of yakking all the time you'd hear a few things. What's

wrong with you?... letting poofs take over a man's sacred place. Wait up.

    (rethinks)

Some bastard just told me that they're gonna 'dose the whole place into the bloody ground tomorrow. What lying bastard would say that to an old man? Thought that that young Mick was one of the hands out of your place. What's he doing driving a dozer anyway? Don't you teach them anything proper?

    (getting panicky)

I can't swim. I ain't gonna sit here in the middle of some great big bloody lake with poofs floating all around a man.

    (finally stops)

SANDY She'll be oke, Pop!

POP (sudden revival) What's going on anyway...?

SANDY Last day, Pop!

PRICKY (hard whisper) Don't tell him.

SANDY Aw, he's got to know.

    (shout back to POP)

You'n'me, we've near done our dash, Pop, so drink up!

    (But POP, deliberately or not – we don't know -- is no longer listening to him. SANDY turns back to PRICKY)

SANDY Last day. Ain't it a fact.

PRICKY   Even most of my mob's buggered off into town today. Nice loyalty to God and country, that is.

SANDY   (sadly) Aw, well, what can you expect?

PRICKY   Who?

> *(They meditate.*
>
> *We now see that this sadness mostly explains the occasional periods of silence they have between them. This characterises, too, their movements of annoyance when either a burst of laughter or of singing comes from inside. One of these bursts of singling comes now.*
>
> *PRICKY puts his ear up against the window by his head. He hears all he wants to and pulls away absolutely horrified.)*

PRICKY   They're singing about Sydney, and that's only one of my favourites, and I don't even know em. What's the world coming to?

SANDY   I wouldn't let 'em get away with that!

PRICKY   Who?

SANDY   You.

PRICKY   Bloody won't either!

SANDY   Knew you wouldn't, Prick.

PRICKY   (but stopping)   What'll I do?

SANDY   ('simple')   Drown 'em out.

> (PRICKY stops at this, looks at SANDY for a shocking display of bad taste)

SANDY   (long-sufferingly)   You drown 'em out, not in-the-lake drown them out. Cripes.

PRICKY   Bloody will, too!

> (He picks up the tune from inside and sings the song loudly, competitively. SANDY joins in when he can and claps time. They take over the song:)

PRICKY:
By the sluggish river Gwyder lived a wicked redback spider
And he was just as vicious as could be.
And the place he camped in was a rusty IXL jam tin.
So he was also just as sticky as could be
Near him lay a shearer snoring; he'd been on the beer all morning
And all the night before and all that very day
And the kooking of the kookers and the noisy showground spruikers
Failed to raise him from the trance in which he lay

*When a crafty looking spieler with a dainty looking sheila
Came along collecting wood to make a fire,
Said the spieler, 'There's a boozer, and he gonna be a loser,
And if he isn't you can christen me a liar.
Wriggle around and keep it, honey, while I pan the mug for money
And we'll have some little luxuries for tea.'
But she answered, 'Don't be silly, you go back and boil the billy;
You can safely leave the mug to little me.'*

*She circled ever nearer, til she reached the dopey shearer
With his pockets bulging, fast asleep and snug.
But she didn't see the spider that was lurking there beside her
For her mind was on the money and the mug.
Now the spider wanted dinner, he was growing daily thinner
He'd been fasting, was as hollow as an urn;
She eyed the bulging pocket, he just darted like a rocket
And bit the spieler's sheila on the stern.*

*Like a flash she raced off squealing, and her clothes began unpeeling
While to hear her yell would make you feel forlorn;
On the bite one hand was pressing while the other was undressing
And she reached the camp the same as she was born.
The shearer pale and haggard woke and back to town he staggered.
He caught the train and gave the booze a rest,
But he'll never know a spider that was camping at the Gywder
Had saved him sixty-seven of the best.*

(In the silence of the victory that follows, SANDY looks up and around the old building. He sighs:)

SANDY Aw, well, it's been a bugger of a place for leading a man astray when you think of it.

PRICKY (sadly) Ain't it a fact.
   (then forcing himself)
Not as bad as the Imperial at Chillagoe. Fair dinkum, I was standing at the bar there once. I remember it was on a Satdee as right as rain…

(MICK returns with a crateful of bottles carefully nestling in his arms. They look at this appreciatively. But he huddles them to himself protectively.)

MICK (defiance) Mother's milk for the morning, orright?

POP (sudden fighting words) What're you doing 'dosing in a working man's pub, ya mug?

MICK (ignoring him) Johnno turned up yet?

PRICKY Who?

(This could be diversionary, because at this time SANDY casually reaches for a bottle, opens it with a multipurpose hunting knife)

MICK Hey, hands off me breakfast!

SANDY   No worries.

>   *(and hands the bottle up to him to have a swig. This largesse of gesture is very hard to refuse even though the bottle belongs to MICK. MICK has to give in and start an inevitable chain reaction of passing around all his bottles. He doesn't realise this as yet' for now, he sits and shares swigging contentedly, while SANDY keeps the bottle supply going)*

MICK   (justification) Johnno owes me boodle anyway.

SANDY   We was just saying about worse pubs than this old bastard ever was. Some were rough as guts in an autopsy.

>   *(POP digs him in the ribs with his foot)*

SANDY   ('replying') Pubs as rough as the old lady's knees!

POP   Ain't they ever, an' I oughta know. Reminds me about the time Snuffler Oldfield's missus was giving birth. The nurse came out and said, 'You've got a baby, Mr Oldfield', then a bit later, 'You've got another baby, Mr Oldfield'. 'Christ, nurse,' he said, 'Don't touch her again! She could be full of them!'
>   *(thinks sagely, before carry on just when they go to drink again)*

That there bloody old Snuffler Oldfirld was one of the Galloping Joneses breed; I can't remember whether or not he was a contemporary. There are thousands of stories about him. You know how they shift them from one character to another.
>   (goes on)

Here's one that I can remember. The cattle rushed every night and Snuffler used to be out risking his life while the boss and the jackeroos and all the silvertails were back in camp, safely up a tree. So one night away went the cattle again and the boss and all of them are up the tree. The boss said, 'My God, poor old Snuffler, he's out there amongst them'. The cattle turned and all raced back through the camp, under the tree, and the manager yelled out, 'Where are you, Snuffler?'

'One limb above you, boss.'

MICK   Yeah, well, talking of the rottenest pub... what about the old Landsborough at Camberweal? That must be one of them if you ask me, straight up. There was that time I was in a terrific blue there. Doug Harris was with us, he walks in and spots a fellow from behind the bar and he says, 'You were a mongrel provo bastard' and up with a bar stool and let it go at him.

Well, that was all the bar needed; they all just wanted an excuse to start! In the struggle I get knocked out through the swing doors, so I flies back in and as soon as I got in some buggerlugs hit me and out I flies again!

So I though next time I'm not getting caught like that, so I crawled in under the swing doors on my hands and knees, and bugger me dead if a fellow doesn't sink a boot into me. Rolled me over and then a couple of blokes walked all over me.

I got out through the swing door and I says to m'self, 'It's too rough for you in there; stay out'. So I watched it from over the top of the swing doors. Well, bugger me again, I reckon three times out of three those swing doors hit me. I wasn't meant to be in there.

     (then indicating inside pub)

We ought to get in there. Some mad city toff in there's laid a tenner on the bar for whoever comes up with the best bit of bullsh. You blokes'd have no problem.

SANDY   A tenner?

MICK   A tenner.

SANDY   Naw, not worth it.

MICK   Not worth it? That sort of bullshit would get you that tenner. That's what I'm saying.

PRICKY   Not even worth a man clearing his throat to whistle up McIlroy's prize bull to the sheep dip.

SANDY   (agreeing) Flamin' insult, really. Where does a tenner go these days?

MICK   Sorry I mentioned it.

   (Pause)

PRICKY   Course a man could go in there and waltz off with it by telling them the one about how we used to hang on to those bloody buckjumpers.

SANDY   You've never seen a buckjumper in your life.

PRICKY   Didn't I b'jesus! When we used to train buckjumpers, we used to get on them in the yard and get them to buck, and after they'd bucked so long we'd jump off then and let them think they'd won. Rightio, so then we'd saddle them up again, or get on them with the same saddle and they'd buck and we'[d let then win again. At times you'd ride the nearly to the finish, and then you'd leave them, but never ever ride them right out – never ride them till they stopped bucking.

Of course there was a few of them there we didn't have to leave; they left us. There'd be an argument between the boys whether we'd left the horse or the horse left us. Course you'd never ever admitted you got thrown. You'd say, 'Oh, I slipped as I was getting off.'

We used to mount all the buckjumpers in the middle of the ring, and this is the way we used to hold them. We use to screw up one ear and get it in our teeth.

    (with contortionistic display)

You'd have the other hand up round underneath the neck, and have the other ear screwed down; you'd have hold of the halter, the twitch down there, like with your hands and the rope. On hand up here with this ear screwed down, you have the other ear screwed up and in your teeth. See? Then you'd jump on the let the whole bloody lot go!

    (shouting to POP's foot nudging him again:)

That's no bull either.!

POP   (getting in before accused of being irrelevant) This horse was a terrible horse to catch, you know. There were four or five fellow running around trying to catch him, running round backwards and forwards around the paddock.

The boss says, 'Do you know this horse?'

'Yes, boss.'

'Can you catch him?'

'I've caught him for the last twelve months, boss.'

'How do you catch him?'

'I got down on my hands and knees and I crawled towards him, and you know why I done that? Well, as I crawls towards him he's starting to think he might have hobbles on, and they must be pestering and annoying him and I was going to take them off. As I crawled closer and closer to him he just stood there and he's worrying about those hobbles, his feet are getting sorer. Finally I played around with his feet, nice and quietly, and then I grabbed him. Yelled out to the other fellows to get a bridle. No trouble, it was the only way to catch him, boss.'

MICK (getting up) Struth, if that Johnno doesn't get here soon, I'll be broker than when I was last looking in the mirror...

>   *(With agitation he goes inside again. They watch him before)*

PRICKY   I heard about that Landsborough at Camooweal Mick mentioned. There was one like that, I reckon, around the Torrens Creek area. Can't remember its name, but I went to that last race meeting they had around that area. Won't ever forget that in a while   Gawd!... during the afternoon Uncle Dick had been boozing up at the bar when he came back to our camp, tanked to the eyeballs. He said that some ringer had been threatening to beat him up. A bit after this he wandered out into the night and flaked out on the ground some little way from the tent. One of the aunts coming back from the toilet came across him lying there, and remembering what he had said earlier, jumped to the conclusion that he had been caught up with by that ringer.

'Poor Dick has been bashed up,' she announced as soon as she got to the tent. Uncle Bill, also with a few beers under his belt jumped up in a rage, 'I'll get the bastard that did', and charged out into the night.

Heading across the flat he tripped over Dick.

'There you are, you rotten bastard', Bill shouted and started to put the boots into Dick's ribs, fist one side then the other.

Near morning old Dick was staggering around the camp holding his sides. 'Some bugger really got me last night and really did me over.'

SANDY C'arn, they were just knocking you off the perch. I'll tell you how I got caught. We were in this bush pub, and everyone was talking about how much you could drink in one go. This fellow said, 'I'll bet anyone that me and my mate can drink a five gallon barrel dry in one go, me taking one long swig and then him'.

Everyone started putting money down and the publican handed over a barrel to the bloke. Instead of tapping the bung out he got hold of a hammer and knocked the whole top out. Then he took a long, long drink, but it wasn't that much. Then he said, 'Now I'll get my mate', and he went out and brought his horse in.

We all lost that bet for sure.

POP What?

> *(SANDY ignores POP's boot nudging him and opens another of MICK's bottles.*
>
> *As he is doing so, JOHNNO comes along. He is surly and worst for wear)*

JOHNNO Seen Mick by any chance?

PRICKY Who?

SANDY What happened to you, Johnno, y'old bastard?

JOHNNO Would you believe it? Bloody snake. Come off me bike. Seen Mick?

PRICKY Mick who?

SANDY   Johnno, you get into more strife than Galloping Jonesy, straight up.

JOHNNO   Who's he when he's home?

SANDY   Only Galloping Jonesy.

JOHNNO   Not the Galloping Jonesy…?!

SANDY   Same one.

JOHNNO   Never heard of him.

SANDY   You never heard of Galloping Jonesy?

JOHNNO   Never in me life.

SANDY   Aw, pull this one. It plays God Save the Queen.

JOHNNO   It'd want to do something useful for a change.

SANDY   Yeah, well… I'll tell you about Galloping Jonesy. He walked into the pub in Georgetown one night and Treacle MacFarlane was there. Everyone got out except Treacle, who didn't know him. Galloping Jonesy said to him, 'When I walk into the pub everyone gets out.'
Treacle said, 'Who are you, mate?'
'Galloping Jones, and who are you?'
'Treacle MacFarlane.'

'And you're not going to get out?'

'No,' he says, 'When everyone else gets out, I stay.'

'And why do you think you can stay?'

'Because I can fight.'

'You want to fight, mate?'

'Yes.'

'Well, you just met your Waterloo.'

Well, they fought for hours and hours, but they couldn't beat one another.

(stops as though finished)

JOHNNO   I don't get it.

SANDY   Who said there was anything to get?
     (and then carries on)

He was a real joker, Galloping Jonesy was. One of the best. No one could put it over him. Even drunk he could take the whole bar on and they couldn't beat him, and to ride a bad horse and things like that they reckon he was terrific.

He used to punch cattle off one place, go past two or three places then sell them. That same night those cattle would be gone again and sold somewhere else. They reckon he was terrible. He didn't want the money or anything; it was just in him. If he saw an iron gate on a property while going through, that night he'd come back and the gate would be gone. If he saw an empty forty-four-gallon drum sitting there, even if it was no good for him, he'd go and pick it up.

One time ago they handcuffed him, because he had killed another man's cow for beef and the coppers rode onto him. So what they done is they cut the brand out to take as evidence. That night, taking him into town, they was sleeping there, the police and the tracker fellow. Galloping Jonesy, he gave them a few rums and when they was sound asleep, he went off and got another hide and he came back and took the police hide and left the fresh hide there, all rolled up, and he put it in the bag and everything.

The next day they took him into town and tried him for stealing. Anyway they got through the evidence and they pulled the hide out to show the brand, and it was one of Galloping Jonesy's own brand!

POP (suddenly lucid) Galloping Jonesy?! He didn't even rate! There used to be an old chap at Mossman, Danny, and he was a terrible strong man. Every now and then he'd get on the grog and he'd say, 'Now well look for a bit of fun'. He'd look out and there'd be…

(stops there. They wait but nothing more. Finally:)

JOHNNO (not impressed) Mike around did you say?

PRICKY Who?

JOHNNO I could use the few red cents he owes me.

SANDY He just went inside looking for a tenner.

JOHNNO (brightening) What'll you have when I find him?

SANDY (indicating bottles, coyly) Well, we were trying to save these for breakfast…

JOHNNO Say no more. Mick'll come good.

(goes to go inside but is stopped by:)

SANDY   Tell you what, Johnno, while you're at it in there tell 'em the one I told about Galloping Jonesy. You never know how many tenners are floating around in there.
   (as explanation)
Big knobs. More money than you could shake a red-bellied at.

JOHNNO   (catching on) No sweat.

(and hurries inside)

PRICKY   Why don't you go in and tell it yourself?

SANDY   Me? In front of a tenner? A man's nerves'd shatter.

PRICKY   (the realist) Yeah, the bloody shakes. They always come at the wrong time.

SANDY   Any rate, a man wouldn't even understand what them city big notes are on about half the time, so how are they gonna understand what we're on about, you tell me that.

PRICKY   (now really depressed) You don't know if that tenner's bullshit or not. The sooner they flood the joint out, the better.

(Long pause)

SANDY   (brooding) Mind you, some lucky bugger ought to rescue that tenner before the tide gets it. How would you reckon this one would go…? Tom Doyle, he was elected to the Kanowna Council. The matter before the house was government aid to have the local water supply dam enlarged as it was too small to supply the needs of a growing town.

Tom was on his feet. 'Yes, it is too small; I could piss half way across it'

Then came the voices of all the other councillors, 'Mr Doyle, Mr Doyle, you're out of order!'

'Yes, bedad, and if I was in order I could piss the whole way across.'

PRICKY   Might be in with a chance. Course, you might have to compete with me telling the one about the mad Irishman Michael Cody who had made a bit of money on the goldfields and he had a new hotel built at West Northam. Northam is about sixty miles east of Perth. This time he'd been in Perth doing business and was standing on the railway platform. The Kalgoorlie Express was just ready to shove off and he was discussing some matters with the brewers.

The guard blew his whistle and waved his flag but old Michael was still talking to these people when the train went off. He shouted, 'Stop the train! Stop the train for Michael Cody of the Grand Hotel, Northam!'

However, they didn't stop the train.

SANDY   You're right. He was a bit of a character, alright. But do you know the greatest character I ever come across? Fred Silas's wife.

PRICKY   Whose Silas's wife?

SANDY   Fred. Fred Silas's wife. She used to come out on the bus. She was a little skinny sort married to a half cast called Fred

Silas and she was very proud of being Fred Silas's wife. She never called herself Mrs Silas, she was always Fred Silas's wife. Well, that old bus, it's a wonder they didn't have to put elastic sides on it, the amount of people it used to carry. Nobody had any cars those days; we were always broke. Coming home at night it would have all these tribal fellows and drunks and Fred Silas's wife.

I remember one night, she was standing up there, drunk, and says, 'Case anyone here don't know me, I'm Fred Silas's wife'.

Oh yes, everybody knows her, but nobody wants to say, the state she's in. So she looks around and she sees Bernie Stone: 'That you there, Bernie?'

Well, quite a few of them were sober this night, I don't know why, and she says, 'You going to have a drink of wine with me, Bernie?'

'No thanks, Daphne.'

'Don't call me Daphne. I'm Fred Silas's wife.'

'All right. Fred Silas's wife.'

She says, 'You won't drink with me, ay? You too stuck up, ay? Yeah, well, I could tell a few things about you Bernie Stone.'

Then she started dragging up his past to all the bus. Everyone's trying to make himself as small and inconspicuous as possible. When she'd finished with old Bernie, she looks around and there's Wally Peters. 'That you, Wally Peters? You know who I am?'

'Yes. Fred Silas's wife.'

'Have a drink with me, Wally?'

'No, no thanks, Daphne, I don't feel like it.'

So she started on [poor old Wally's history and we thought it would never end. Then she saw Rex Jones, 'That you there, Rex? You going to have a drink with me, Rex?'

'My bloody oath I am,' says Rex, 'Gimme the bottle!'

POP   What?!

SANDY   Real characters, Pop!

POP   Real characters? One comes to me mind alright was the old bastard I met at the post office. The postie had told me that he owned Ned Kelly's plough, so I asked him about it. 'Are you the man who has Ned Kelly's plough?'

'Yes, that's me and would you believe it, it has a wooden blade. Now some people wouldn't believe that.'

So I says, 'Do you know any songs about Ned Kelly?'

'Songs? Well, I've got a muzzle-loading six shooter of his; have you ever heard of one of those?'

'I haven't. But do you know any songs about Ned?'

'And I've got an old Roman sword belonging to Ned Kelly, about this long, with an old English string handle. Now would you believe it.'

At this point old Jackson, who had been listening to all this, and had never seen the other bloke in his life, shouted out, 'Tell us about those songs your old man sung about Ned Kelly when he came home drunk!'

The other bloke with Ned Kelly's wooden plough just stared at him for a bit, and then went on to tell us other Ned Kelly wonders he owned.

A few days later I see him again and I go, 'Have you remembered any songs about Ned Kelly yet?'

'No, but they might be in my car; I've got all sorts of things in there, sandsoap and things like that old Ned swore by…'

SANDY   Yeah, but he was nothing compared to a

>*(stops when MICK comes back out and casts a sorrowful eye at the dwindling supply of bottles)*

MICK   Johnno come back yet?

PRICKY   Who?

SANDY   That tenner gone yet?

(MICK shakes his head forlornly, sits down to a swig)

SANDY   As I was saying about that Ned Kelly character. He was nothing compared to a bloke I used to work with nature. His best idea was that of walking from Cairns to the tip of Cape York; I suppose it would be a bit better than five hundred miles. He said it would be no trouble; he was not scared of a bit of exercise. He got all his stuff ready for the big trek, and then found that no one would drive him the two miles out to the main road, so he gave the whole idea away and caught the next train south.

PRICKY   While you're on about on the track and wives, you remind a bloke of the old Afghan camel driver and his mad missus I once heard about. He was called Galloping too. The Galloping Ghan. He was fairly well known in northern New South Wales and southern Queensland; all around that area. His territory ranged out to Burke, and the fellow who told me about it came from Burke.

Galloping Ghan's wife was a very good looking sort, and a fellow she'd known for some time came by and she offered him tea and they finally ended up in an immoral embrace on the couch. Old Galloping G. walked in on them, and his wife caught sight of him and she shouted out, 'Rape! Rape!'

He said, 'What for you cry when I see your big arse lift up?'

   (He sails on regardless of others objecting to the bad taste)

Then there was this old coot called Bloody Old Bill, too. His real name was Norm Brown. No idea why they used to call him Bloody Old Bill. Anyhow, he was a great one for fighting too, especially with a bit of O.P. in him. I recall one time there was a bit of a party going on, dancing and that, and in came Bloody Old Norman Bill full of good spirits. All the woman and kids go out of the place very smartly, and then he threw all the men out, and then one by one he threw out every bit of crockery, all the plates and cups and pans, and then he started on the furniture, all the chairs and tables and the sideboard, the lot.

Finally there was nothing left in the place but the old rood stove. He tried to grab it, but it was red hot. So there he was, nothing at all in the place but him and the stove, and the stove had him beat. It was about the only thing that ever tossed him.

MICK Jeez, you speak a lot of bullsh.

SANDY I don't know about that.

POP (as though suddenly remembering MICK) What's he doing going round saying he's gonna 'dose me pub down?

MICK (stung) Shit, I've already told him a hundred times.

PRICKY Who?

SANDY Told you he don't hear a word.

MICK (agitated) I dunno where that bloody Johnno's got to.

PRICKY Who?

SANDY He's just been here, as a matter of fact.

MICK Where?

SANDY About where you're sitting, I reckon. Matter of fact, he just went inside looking for you.

MICK (suspiciously) I didn't see him.
   (then cunningly)
Who's shout anyway?

(when all falls silent, he knows he might as well get up and go inside to look for JOHNNO)

SANDY Hey, Mick, while you're buying, nice of you, I'll share the tenner with you if you hit them with the one about the pub with the bell and the mad landlady with the broom.

MICK Go in and tell it yourself.

SANDY Naw, I wouldn't know where to start yakking.

MICK (sudden shout) For crying out loud, did you see that?

PRICKY Who?

MICK Bloody big rat size of e backside of a few barmaids I know!

PRICKY Been here all afternoon, that has.

SANDY Thought it was a bit of rat's turd on the ground at first, but it turned out to be the rat without the turd.

PRICKY We was saying them
    (indicates city slickers inside)
in there must've brought it with 'em. It's too small for one of the local variety...

Years ago I was riding around the Coolgarra country, and Jimmy Stone and I came on this old camp. In the distance you could see all these tins gleaning and shining, and when we got closer we saw thousands of old jam tins and syrup tins stacked up neatly.

We were talking to the old boy there and he said, 'The price of tin's going up. There's to be a big shortage and that's why I'm saving all these tins.' Silly bugger.

We looked around a bit and there's a kangaroo rat hanging by the neck. He'd been hanging up for a fortnight by the smell of him.

'You been having trouble with kangaroo rats?'

'Yes,' he says, 'Yes, they're a trouble all right, them bloody things. All night long sniffing and snorting around the camp. All you can hear is thump thump, squeak squeak. I tried poisoning them, but they're too cunning. I tried shooting them but they dodge bullets, they do. I didn't know what to do about them. I managed to catch one. I give him a fair trial. I tried him and found him guilty of jumping around the camp all night and keeping me awake. I sentenced him to death and I hung him.

'See that big blackboard up there? Can you read what's on it? KANGAROO RATS BEWARE. DON'T LET THIS HAPPEN TO YOU.

I hung him up there and that night thousands of them came hopping around, squeaking and thumping. Then they just stopped, and they started to read that notice on the board. The minute they read it they just wheeled around and took off, and you could hear them thumping over the ridge. They haven't annoyed me since.'

MICK Fair dinkum you mob'd make the biggest damn liar in the world spit chips, you would.

SANDY Never met him, but I was once in Blinman in South Australia at the old copper mine. I was installing some machinery and I met an old Irishman, Mick Carrick, who was a great stretcher of the odd yarn or two. He had been a bullock driver and one evening at the hotel, I put a couple of pints of beer into old Mick and this is the story he told me:

'I had the best team of bullocks that ever put their necks into a yoke. I was carting wool one trip from Bullcamatta in Hergott Springs. It's a long track and on the way I had to cross Coopers Creek. Well, Coopers Creek in flood time is impossible, you just simply can't go past, but at this time it was only eighteen inches deep.

'So we arrived at the southern side of Coopers Creek and I pulled up the bullocks. I said, "Whoa, me boys, whoa now; you've got a job in front of you". I walked into the water and it was just about up to me knees. I went back and walked around the team, and mind you, the team of bullocks I had there were the best team that had ever put their necks into a yoke, like I said. By God, they were a fine team of bullocks.

'Well, I went around and I told each bullocks and there were twenty-two of them in the team. I told 'em just exactly what I wanted of them. I goes up to the off side leader, Big Baldy, a marvellous bullock, a real friend of mine, and I stood off and gave a little bit of a crack with the old whip. I never lashed my bullocks; I'd just drop the lash onto them; they didn't need any more than that.

'I shouted, "Come on, old boys, gee old Baldy" and they put their necks in the yoke and they entered the water, and they pulled.

'I walked alongside them, and I shouted to them, telling them what a difficult job they had to get through the water. Eventually we came up on the other side and I said, "Whoa, me boys, steady now, have a spell!" I turned around and I looked back, and you may not believe it, it's no bloody lie, but that team of bullocks of mine had pulled Coopers Creek ten chains off its bloody course! That's the godsbold flea-bitten truth, that is. They were a damn fine team of bullocks, they were.'

(SANDY cracks another bottle without asking, much to MICK's disgust)

MICK   Hey, fair go!

SANDY   (diversion) If you catch the thirst going around
 (indicates the racket inside the pub)
in there, Mick, you could always tell 'em the one about the wind at Goldsmith's Creek. There weren't any rats; it was too windy.

MICK   Oh, bull.

SANDY   No, straight up. It was terrible windy place that Forsyth. When I was there a few years ago, I mentioned it to Pat Haigh, and he said the wind was even worse a few miles further out at a place called Goldsmith Creek. According to him the wind was so strong it used to blow dogs off their chains, and a man could only work about an hour a day.
'Why would that be?', I asked, expecting some scientific answer and Pat Haigh said, 'Because he spends the rest of his time chasing his hat'.

MICK   Listening to you lot worse than trying to get me loan back from Johnno. Inside, is he...?.

(He goes to go off inside)

SANDY (stopping him)   Don't forget breakfast, Mick!

MICK   What about breakfast?

SANDY (tapping MICK's now near-gone bottle crate)   When you donated this, you said remind you about yer breakfast stash.

MICK (sourly) Stash? I'd need a bank vault.

PRICKY   We're just saying.

(MICK goes off inside.

JOHNNO comes out almost ridiculously soon after MICK has gone in. He stands and, in unison with them, watches the movements of the rat off the verandah)

JOHNNO (finally) Seen Mick?

SANDY   He was just this minute askin' about you.

JOHNNO   Well, he'd better front up soon. I need to wet the whistle badly.

(SANDY magnanimously motions him to sit and help himself to MICK's stash. JOHNNO needs no second asking)

JOHNNO Ask bloody Mick for a small ale and you wouldn't see a rain cloud for years

SANDY That tenner gone yet?

JOHNNO What tenner's that?

PRICKY (fierce whisper to SANDY) He's taken it off!

JOHNNO (regardless) You wouldn't believe how much lying's going on in there. There's so much bullsh, flooding'll only turn this place into one big dunny drain.

SANDY Just goes to show what money does. Better off without it.

PRICKY (toasts to:) To free beer!

(pause to savour the taste of it, then:)

SANDY They might come another tenner if they heard about the old chap who used to be out our way. Now there was a terrible liar for you, if ever there was one.

POP Eh? What?!

SANDY Liars, Pop!

POP (getting in, gleefully) Don't give me liars, son! You remember what a rotten liar that George was? It didn't matter what you said or did, he had done it before you and better. Like that there time when we were talking to him about the saw, one of those saws that have wheels attached, and you walk them up to the tree.

He had never heard of one in his life, because it had to be explained to him in detail, but having once grasped what it was all about, he straightway became an expert. A few minutes later someone remarked how dangerous these saws could be if the blade broke while they were going; in fact a bit of the saw could take a bloke's head off with no trouble at all.

So right out of the blue George says, 'Yes, that happened to me once when I was using one of those cows of things, and a piece went into my forehead right there', and he pointed to the middle of his forehead and said, 'Can't you see the scar?'

His head was as smooth as a baby's bum and we all said we couldn't see a thing.

'Look,' he said, jabbing with his finger, 'Right next to where I got shot with the .303 bullet'.

We all said, give's us a break, George, we couldn't see that either, but it didn't worry George… 'Ah,' he said, 'that's the wonders of plastic surgery'.

JOHNNO   If Mick turns up tell him I'm looking for him inside, orright?

SANDY   (after him) You tell 'em that one Pop just said.

> *(Pause while they look expectantly at the pub's door after Johnno has gone inside. But there is no unusual burst of laughter that he might have told one of their yarns for a tenner)*

PRICKY   If he told it, it went down like a dose of cod's.

SANDY   Bugger probably forgot the punch line or something. Driving dozers does that to a man's brain.

POP   What?!

SANDY   (picks up conversation to PRICKY)   How'd you say you went at the Torrens Creek races that time?

PRICKY   Go? That flamin' horse was alright. It would've walked it in if that skinny looking drongo of a jockey hadn't broken down in the straight the first time he tried lifting the whip. Y'know my old Dad always claimed that the only bloke who ever made money following horses was the ploughman.

When I was a bit of a kid the old man was ploughing in the paddock and this joker came along. He was looking for a bloke who was reputed to be very strong. The old man was ploughing out garden patch which was a swamp about two to three acres long, and a good one too.

The old man said to the fellow, 'Yes, he lives about three miles in that direction' and he lifted up the plough in one hand and pointed with it.

SANDY   Yeah, you can talk about being riding and going astray. There was that time Vic was going to take a horse and follow in the tracks of Kennedy the explorer. He got into all his cowboy gear and got himself photographed with somebody's old hack, gazing romantically across the plains, in someone's back yard. He managed to get the photo into one of the Sydney papers. It was real explorer stuff.

As you may know Kennedy started off from around Cardwell on the east coast and more or less followed the coast up all the way to where he was killed.

We asked Vic whether he would be starting right from Cardwell, and he said no, he would be starting from Normanton. Well, Normanton is five hundred miles to the west, and he was going to head straight up the middle of the peninsula from there, so he really wouldn't be anywhere near the track taken by Kennedy. So we asked him why, if his expedition was to follow in the footsteps of Kennedy, he was going five hundred miles to the west, and the silly bugger said it would be easier riding out there!

Anyway once he got himself in the papers that was enough. He didn't have to make the trip then.

> *(MICK returns this time. He is visibly getting desperate. He can't find JOHNNO; he is running out of money; he is out of his depth with the city-slicker developers inside; his bottle supply for the morning all too obviously dwindled. He has a good whine:)*

MICK   Jesus, what a bastard of a life. Johnno won't show. You can't get near the bar for blokes speaking with plums in their north-and-souths. Every bastard's trying to make a bloke do funny turns or something. A couple of the pricks are flashing the big ones into Shirl's shell-like, and she put a man on a promise tonight. A man can't even buy her a beer to settle her down while bloody Johnno's avoiding a man like the bloody plague. To top it all, the beer's gone warm as mother's milk in a heat wave   Life stinks!

PRICKY (after pause)   How'd you go?

SANDY   How's that tenner going in there?

MICK   (surly)   What tenner?

PRICKY   Who?!

    (then to their disgust of him keeping saying that)

Hey, Sandy, you could get Mike to go in there and tell 'em about old Chicko.

SANDY   (perking up)   Rightio!   Here's one, Mick, for the tenner and Shirl!

MICK   (suspicious)   What about the bloody warm beer?

SANDY   They'll lash you out with buckets of ice with this one!
    (now with MICK's attention:)

Old Chicko was a travelling magician who used to go from country pub to country pub all over Queensland, all over Australia for all I know, doing a variety of ancient tricks and passing around the hat. As a rule the publicans didn't mind letting him have the use of the lounge for half an hour or so. It was a bit of entertainment for the drinkers and cost them nothing.

Some of the tricks were so ancient that they started to collapse before he got through them.

The best story I knew about him happened one evening in the Redlynch pub. He was busy pulling strings of dirty hankies out of an apparently empty tube when the false lining of it slid out onto the floor. He looked at it sadly, bent down and picked it up and stuffed it back where it had come from, 'I'd be buggered without that.'

MICK   That's not going to get any tenner.

SANDY   Hey, they're from the big smoke. What'd they know about a man being on Shirl's promise?

MICK   Be buggery, you're right! Here goes…!

   (he chuffs off inside again)

SANDY   He's going to murder that Johnno when he finds him.

POP   (renewed burst) You gotta get him before the mug comes to 'dose a man's only pub into the ground!

SANDY   Mick is!

PRICKY   Who?

SANDY   Don't you start.
   (then)
He used to be a bit of the old wild Irishman, Mick did, before the sheilas got hold of him. Shame really. The trouble is blokes don't take sheilas as they come.

PRICKY   Who?

SANDY   All I'm saying is there's no doubt about the way women can get you into strife, especially if you get mixed up with too many of them. A bloke that I know… nickname's Hoppy… took up with this Chinese sheila at the meatworks. They're sex mad out there. They were going along all right till Hoppy's wife gets to hear about it. Someone had tripped over Hoppy and this Chinese sort under a mango tree along the road. Was his missus mad.

Hoppy came in for lunch next day and she bangs the plate down in front of him and nothing else.

'Where's the knife and fork?,' he says.

She just gives him a dirty look and says, 'Why don't you try chopsticks?'

(POP queries him with a nudge of the foot again)

POP   What?!

SANDY   Strange sheilas, Pop!

(It is JOHNNO who re-emerges this time. He hurries in from around the side of the pub. He could be running from, or looking for, MICK)

JOHNNO   You blokes wouldn't be pulling a man's pisser about Mick, would you?

PRICKY   Who?

SANDY   (really disappointed with JOHNNO's lack of beer) Don't tell me you couldn't get near the bar neither?

JOHNNO   Mick's not in there.

SANDY   Don't tell me some other bugger's won that tenner.

JOHNNO   A bloke's looked high and low in there. He's not even behind the bar up Shirl's skirt. Hope the greasy mug's fingers turn green and drop off. If they don't haul me off for vagrancy, the mad house'll get me. Bloody Mick.

PRICKY   Who?

POP   (jolting to action)   Me? Well, I'll tell yer if you want to listen…I used to be a hydroambulationist. You can ask what that is and I'll tell you it's walking through water and I'll fight any sod who says it ain't. It is something entirely new that I brought out myself. You've got to see it to believe it. And you know what? I appeared at the Adelaide Show once and I gave a six hour show and asked for 48 quid and they gave me 50. The first act I do is walking through water reading a book. Next I carry an umbrella and a hat in the other hand, then change hands and walk backwards. Next I walk sideways with a mouth organ, then I walk the other way breathing in and out. I said I'd walk across Bass Strait in forty hours but no one dared challenge me…

> *(JOHNNO doesn't stay to listen to any more of this. He exits trying to catch MICK around the other side of the pub)*

POP (undeterred) I walk in water and it comes just above me waist. I bend my head slightly and start squeezing a few notes out on me mouth organ, and the water acts as a megaphone. I play 'When I Grow Too Old to Sleep' and 'There's a Long Trail Awaiting', and several others I could mention.

Who asked what's the diff between treading water and walking through water? Treading water requires great manual exertion, the legs going out sideways. Walking in water the way I do requires no exertion at all.

I can pirouette on the tips of my toes in any depth of water, lay on an angle in any depth of water, turn north, east, south and west, kneel in salt water and don't sink, and also various other items too numerous to mention. I will not divulge the secrets. I keep them in the family.

(MICK comes out through pub's front door; takes a doleful look at his near nonexistent supply for the morning, has quick look down sides of the pub for JOHNNO)

MICK   Mongrel, that Johnno. Someone said they saw him lurking out here.

PRICKY   Who?

SANDY   Anyone knocked off that tenner yet?

MICK   I've posted scouts on every door and every flaming window in there. I've swung from the light so I could cop any bird's eyeful of the bludger. Now they want to charge me for it. I said you'd be bloody lucky, cocko, I ain't got enough to scratch m'bum with, let alone to fix any bloody crook light fitting probably broke before I climbed on. And that bloke who copped it underneath, I ain't paying for any ambulance; he shoulda known how jumped out of the way like I did. Okay, I said, charge me for manslaughter but wait til I finished those few lousy beers that bloody Johnno owes a man. Life stinks!
   (pauses)
Y'know, I know Johnno's not in there, but it's getting like I'd swear he ain't in there. Knowing he's a bit deaf, I even asked Shirl to whisper his name aloud. Shit, who can't hear a foghorn like her lest he's not wanting to?

SANDY   Tried to dunny out back?

MICK   Course I tried the... Bejesus, you might be right!

(hurries off around the other side of the pub to JOHNNO)

POP We had this stockman working here, Johnny Colombo, and I sent him out to find a mare that had escaped. I'd forgotten all about him, working around the yards, but in the evening he finally got back with that mare there.

'You found that mare all right then?'

'Yes, boss. I found her way over there. Didn't you see the smoke signal I sent up to let you know I'd found it?'

Didn't I see that smoke signal? That bloody smoke signal burnt off most of the Gulf country and we fought it for four months.

> *(JOHNNO bursts back onto the verandah from the side that MICK has just left by)*

JOHNNO Don't tell me I missed him again!

PRICKY Who?

JOHNNO Any of you seen Mick come by here?

SANDY You notice if that tenner's still there?

> *(But JOHNNO pauses only to take a quick swig of MICK's bottle he left behind before dashing off around the other side)*

SANDY (shout to POP) Chinaman, was he?

PRICKY Who?

SANDY (still to POP) With the mare? Nothing's off like Sam Wong.

    (but POP has gone 'off' again; even so)

Remember him? That time my Wendy first meets him? She turned up at his house looking all prim and proper and clutching her big black bag which looked as though it might have been full of copies of the Salvo's 'Watch Tower', but actually contained her tape recorder. Sam must have taken her for a Jehovah's Witness, and the conversation went something like this:

'This where Sam Wong lives?'

'It might be.'

'Do you know if he's at home?'

'Don't know.'

'Listen, are you Sam Wong?'

'No.'

'Bullshit.'

'Come in.'

    (MICK comes bursting back in from the other side of the pub).

MICK I'll kill the mug, so help me!

PRICKY Who?

    (He goes to dash off again, but stops by his supply, and with no hope:)

MICK At least I know you blokes have the decency to replenish a man's life blood when you see it drained off...

(takes off)

SANDY (after him) No worries, Mick! You just snag that tenner and Bob's your uncle…!

POP (about MICK) Here, what's the dill going to 'dozer down me pub for?

SANDY A dam, Pop!

POP Damn what?

SANDY A dam lake!

POP What flaming lake? Funny thing is I was talking to some codger not long ago and he was on about a lake or something. He was going on about a missing river around here or somewhere. I dunno. I never heard about a missing river around here. What a thing, to knock down a good pub for a missing river.

> *(There is a silence, while they ponder the passing of the pub.*
> *There is a burst of singing from inside. PRICKY hums along to it sadly and then sings along)*

PRICKY
Oh, where is the lady whose dark eyes
I so often kissed and caressed?
She is sleeping under far-distant skies
With her head on some other man's breast.
Though she said my life she would ere share,

It seems she's forgotten our love so soon
But a man can't care when it's so hard to keep square
On the banks of the Reedy Lagoon.

> *(Renewed silence. The three of them remain static in contemplation and take no notice of the following sequence around them:*
>
> *MICK and JOHNNO – both of them madly running – dash in and out in a series of foot-banging, floorboard-rattling near misses. This starts with:*
>
> *JOHNNO dashes out of the door, sees MICK isn't on the verandah, turns and plunges back inside.*
>
> *MICK dashes around from the right side of the pub, up onto the verandah and into pub through the door.*
>
> *JOHNNO enters from left side of pub and hurries inside by the back door.*
>
> *MICK dashes out of pub door and hurries around the left side of the building,*
>
> *JOHNNO dashes out of the pub door and hurries around the right side of the building.*
>
> *MICK dashes back from around the left side of the pub and runs off around the right side of the pub.*

JOHNNO dashes in from the right side and run in through pub door, then a split second later comes back out of door again and hurries around the left side of the building.

Etcetera.

PRICKY languidly breaks the others' silence, indicates across the yard)

PRICKY   I reckon that might be a local rat after all. Or is it a dog?

SANDY   What's its tail like?

PRICKY   Like a pig's, I guess.

SANDY   What's it sound like?

PRICKY   Like a bucking bronco I once had, I guess.

SANDY   Aw, pack it up.

   (MICK comes back, livid)

MICK   You're all a lot of mongrels.

PRICKY   Who?

MICK   Johnno ain't around here at all.

SANDY   We was only trying to help.

MICK   (at depleted beer) Help? You're termite-ing a man's breakfast. You're denying him his heart starter. You have him whizzing around like a loony while those city-ites are in Shirl's pants. Life stinks! The whole pack of you galoots deserve to get bulldozed tomorrow. No, I tell you what… I ain't waiting for tomorrow!

(He dashes out)

SANDY   (after him) I take it that tenner's gone?

POP   What's he doing?

PRICKY   Who?

SANDY   He's going to 'doze the place in, Pop.

POP   Toldyer I dreamt about some snake 'dozing a man's pub in. How much of a sneaky animal can you get?

(But they sit there placidly, without even looking up, when the bulldozer starts up. It is put crashingly into gear and then becomes louder and louder until its approach becomes deafening.

Fade out)

ACT 2

(By contrast, only the screeching of cockatoos.)

POP, SANDY and PRICKY are where they were.

Suddenly, all hell breaks loose again. MICK comes crashing in flat out from left side of building, dashes across the verandah, disappears around the right side of the building.

JOHNNO follows madly -- almost, but not quite, on his heels.

Then JOHNNO comes crashing in going flat out from the right side of the pub, crosses the verandah and disappears around left side of the pub.

MICK follows madly – almost, but not quite, on his heels.

JOHNNO comes back flat out from the right side of the building across verandah and disappears off around left side of the building.

MICK follows madly – almost, but not quite, on his heels.

MICK comes flying back from the right side and careers past them to off around the left side.

JOHNNO follows madly -- almost, but not quite, on his heels

They are flagging, though.

It all goes dead silent again.

Finally MICK comes back in, takes a beer, sits, swigs, then:)

MICK   Got you going with that 'dozer back there, didn't I?

SANDY   How'd you say that tenner was going?

MICK   What tenner?

SANDY   That tenner

MICK   No tenner.

SANDY   Knock it off.

MICK   There was never no tenner.

SANDY   The real shitheads!

PRICKY   The dirty rotten city-arsed dingoes!
    (then)
Who?

SANDY   They made me cough up me best yarn for nothing!

PRICKY   Same here.

SANDY   Bugger it, I was going to tell 'em about Glen Broughton too.

PRICKY   Who?

SANDY   Not who.

PRICKY   Who's that one, then?

SANDY   Not who!

POP   What?!

SANDY   (losing patience)   The bloody mozzies, what else?

POP   (nodding sagely)   There used to be a lot of pigs in among the mangroves and salt pans back of the farm. One day I was poking around I came across a hut like one of those New Guinea ones. It was built up in a tree, and there was this old joker digging around all the trees and all he had on was a waistcoat.
So I said to him on account of only having on this waistcoat, 'What's the idea of the waistcoat?'
'I've got to have somewhere to keep me matches,' he said.
That did it. I asked him how he handled the mozzies there.
'Well', he said, 'there's three ways you can deal with them. The best way is to keep still and let them get their tusks in and then when they've had a decent feed they'll leave you in peace.

'Now a lot of people get jumping about and all that and it gets the mosquitoes even angrier because their tusks get stuck jammed and keep breaking.

'I reckon the best way to deal with them is to go down to the swamp and roll round in that black mud. When that stuff dries on you, it's like an armour plate, and the mosquito gets his tusk into it and can't get it out and he pulls and pulls and ends up pulling off a wad of about two inches square. Well, when that mosquito gets free he'll fly back to his mates and warn them off you, and that way you'll be left alone.'

MICK (surly admission) Yeah, well, when I said there was no tenner it was fifty not a tenner.

SANDY Joking.

MICK They're city buggers, they wouldn't know the difference.

SANDY (craftily) Well, I was saving up the one where there were three of us, sleeping in a row, when this big boar pig, he walked down the pad and come straight down past my feet, past the middle bloke, and he come right around and looked at the joker on the end. He looked straight in, close on the mosquito net.

I heard, 'Go way! Go on, git!' I heard this; I'd been sound asleep and I thought what in the hell goes on here? I woke up and this fellow on the end, he wasn't game to move, but the bloke in the middle, he said, 'Hey, Les, you better wake up'.

I had a .32 there with me. When I rolled over I could see this pig and he's looking into the net down the end. He was a huge bloody thing. This bloke would say, 'Shoo!' and that pig just walked around a bit then came back and looked in the net again. I thought this is something unusual for a pig; this ain't right. I loaded the rifle and stood up and put one into him. He took off and stopped again, so I put the torch onto him and walked up and put another one into him, and he fell down.

About twenty minutes later back he came, the same bloody pig. He did. He came back and kept looking at this bloke through that bloody net. I thought that's funny. So I put the torch on him and put another couple into him.

It was the same pig, but I don't know why he ever came back. He'd come down along the pad and if he'd wanted to have a look at anybody, I was sleeping right by the entrance. But he walked around me and around the other fellow and got to the bloke on the end, straight up.

He was standing there hitting his tusks nice and slow on the bed and looking into the net. Next morning he was laying there and he had four holes in him.

Can you beat that?

PRICKY (not to be outdone) That's all right about that, but for 50 smackeroos, I might trot out that one about that Nelem. He was a clever goat, he was. One time when we were all living on St Pauls…

> *(He is irrevocably interrupted by JOHNNO creeping back in backward from out of the front door. He casts sneaky looks around both sides of the pub and relaxes until he sees MICK actually there)*

MICK Bastard!

JOHNNO (recovering shock) What's your game?

MICK A man ought to job you!

JOHNNO   What's he on about?

MICK   Hand it over.

JOHNNO   Hand what over?

PRICKY   Who?

MICK   The spondoolix you bludged off me.

JOHNNO   You hand over the spondoolix you bludged off me.

> *(There is a real danger they will actually come to blows, but this is shouted down by PRICKY who suddenly hears singing inside. He listens with his ear to the wall while they wait on him, then shows absolute outrage... almost to the extent of rising to his feet.)*

PRICKY   They're doing it again!

SANDY   Who?

PRICKY   Not who! They're taking a man's song! Who's the stoolie?! Who's the loud mouth!?

SANDY   Who?

PRICKY   Only me one about Charlie Mopps, that's all!

SANDY   Go get 'em, Prick.

PRICKY   Bloody will too!

(He climbs shakily to his feet and sings loudly and defiantly straight at the window. While he does so, MICK and JOHNNO break off and join the drinking circle, but with backs to each other)

PRICKY

A long time ago, twas way back in history
When all we had to drink was nothing but cups of tea
Along came a man by the name of Charlie Mopps
And he invented a beaut brew with the name of hops.

(chorus)
Oh, he should have been an admiral, a sultan or a king
And to his praise we will always stand to sing;
Look what he's done; he's filled us with good cheer,
God bless Charlie Mopps, the inventor of beer!

Oh, the Oceanic, the Barrier Reef and the Federal Hotel
One thing's sure, it's Charlie's brew they all sell
So come on me lucky lads at ten 'clock she stops
For five short seconds let's remember Charlie Mopps!

(chorus)
Oh, he should have been an admiral, a sultan or a king
And to his praise we will always stand to sing;
Look what he's done; he's filled us with good cheer,
God bless Charlie Mopps, the inventor of beer!

Well, Charlie he died, he went to Heaven's door
Up to old St Peter, said, 'Pete, what's the score?'
St Peter looked at Charlie, said, 'Who the hell are you?'
Charlie said, 'Charles Mopps'; St Peter cried, 'Straight through!'

(chorus)
Oh, he should have been an admiral, a sultan or a king
And to his praise we will always stand to sing;
Look what he's done; he's filled us with good cheer,
God bless Charlie Mopps, the inventor of beer!

> *(Gets boos and derisive laughter from inside)*

SANDY   Buggers don't appreciate fine music.

> *(He drowns his disgust with opening another bottle of beer, swigs, hands it on to JOHNNO. JOHNNO goes to have a guzzle but MICK snatches the bottle away)*

JOHNNO   Bash it up your bum then.

MICK   'Bash it up your bum'. Nice and charming.

> *(POP stirs)*

SANDY   (almost alarmed)   Hold it!

MICK   What?

SANDY   Pop moved.

MICK   I didn't see it. You, Pricky?

PRICKY   Who?

(they wait on POP but nothing comes before JOHNNO cannot hold his tongue any longer)

JOHNNO   I said bash it up your quoit, and I meant ram it into your dyke!

POP   (unexpectedly again) You talk about pulling the sorts. I was in a pub in Katherine, and a bit of a brawl started between a couple of blokes. In the middle of it, a girl who must've favoured the other bloke raced up to the first mug and started to kick him in the shins.
He swung around and went to punch her, but one of his friends standing near said, 'You can't do that, you must never hit a lady', so he shook his head and turned his back on her.
She ducked outside and next thing she'd come back in carrying a long metal sign advertising Dunlop rubber. She swung this around her head and went to whack him, and the poor bugger didn't know what to do until his mate said, 'I think it would be all right to hit her now!'

PRICKY   (not to be silenced) Alright, you don't want to hear about Nelem the goat, but did old Alf ever tell you about the fellows that got bogged?
He said out in front of his place were three blokes bogged there for six weeks with this old truck. I reckon that after a fortnight I would have given it away and walked out.

Those poor huggers were starving and they were packing up this truck and revving it back and forwards, building logs under it and jacking it up, but the bastard of a thing still wouldn't move.

Do you know those Estonians up there? There was a big family of them, big women you know, and there was this one woman and she decided to go to Mareeba, walked in from Julatten, must be about thirty miles, to do her shopping.

When she was in Mareeba, she walked around looking for bargains and she bought a wood stove. They must weigh about two hundred pounds, but she just put it up on her head and decided to walk back to Julatten.

Coming back she saw these three drongos who had been bogged for six weeks. She said, 'What are you hanging around here for?'

'We're bogged.'

'Right, well I'll give you a bit of a hand.'

She reached up with one hand, lifted the stove off her head and put it on the ground and she said to this fellow, 'You, you miserable little rat, you get in and you steer it.'

'Do you want me to start it up too, missus?'

'No, dopey, I'm going to lift the wheels up and wheelbarrow it out.'

The other blokes said, 'What will we do?'

And she said, 'You stand back and encourage the other bloke.'

Then she reached down with her big powerful arms and grabbed the truck and there was a sucking sound and she lifted it straight out of that mud and wheelbarrowed it right back onto dry ground.

And one of those who was listening to old Alf's yarn said, 'God, she must have been a two-ton Tessie walking all the way from Mareeba with a wood stove on her head and then wheelbarrowing a truck out like it hadn't been stuck in there for six weeks'.

Old Alf said, 'Aw, that wasn't half of it. I didn't mention the three bags of spuds she'd bought and had on top of the stove.'

POP   (daggers at MICK)   Too much noise and too many machines around the country these days.   Mug larrikins.

SANDY   I've been thinking the ghost of John Brown ought to be worth a fifty, Mick, split. Whatcha reckon…? You know how all them boundary riders' huts are all haunted because in almost every one of them at least one boundary rider has committed suicide.

The poor buggers all commit suicide… well, not all, but it's a sort of professional hazard of being a boundary rider, like. They all knock themselves off. That's why most of the huts are haunted.

This bagman one time went into a boundary rider's hut and he was fooling around, unpacking his gear and whatnot in the dark and there was a storm on The next thing, he bumped into someone in there. That was enough for him; he tore outside and camped out in the rain.

Next morning he met a bloke walking down the road with his swag and he said to him, 'Where did you camp?'

'Oh,, I had a bastard of a camp out in the rain. I went into that bloody boundary-rider's hut up there and there's something in there, I'm telling you.'

Well the first bloke said, 'Yes, I was in there and it frightened the seven bells of hell out of me too! What time were you there?'

'About eight o'clock.'

Of course they found out they'd scared one another.

I don't know whether that originated from a true story or not, but I've heard it polished up. In this version the bloke was getting undressed in the hut and this ghost said, 'I'm a ghost of John Brown' and all this sorta stuff and went on, 'There is only you and me here. Only you and me are here, whoooo.'

And the other fellow there said, 'Yes, and when I find this other bloody boot you'll be here on your own!'

JOHNNO (out of patience) What dyou mean the dough I owe you.

MICK   Don't give me that.

JOHNNO   You owe me.

MICK   You owe me, you mean.

JOHNNO   Hey, I was the one chasing all over this joint after you!

MICK   Bullsh, I was on your hammer!

JOHNNO   I got calluses on me feet to prove it!

MICK   You'll have a thick ear on your head to prove it if you don't watch out.

JOHNNO   (warning) Mate…

MICK   (ditto) Mate…

PRICKY (breaking it up, to SANDY) Why don't you get Pop going on Kidman again, Sandy mate?

SANDY   Gawd no, they'd shove that fifty back into their kicks and you wouldn't see 'em for dust.

PRICKY   For old time's sake, like. Town's going to be too far for him. A man might never hear him going at his Kidman again.

SANDY   What a glutton for punishment.
     (but even so to POP)
Kidman, Pop!

POP   (chuckling) Old Kidman, eh? Don't get me started on him. Struth, they say there was only one time Kidman ever got taken in in all his life That was when this old Chinaman came along and Kidman took a liking to his horse.
'Will you sell this horse?'
'Yes, I sell him all wight, but he no lookee too good.'
Kidman rode around him two or three times.
'He looks all right to me. I'll buy him.'
'All wight, but he still no lookee too good.'
So Kidman gave the old fellow five pounds, and took the horse home.
Next day he came back and he says to the Chinaman, 'Hey, listen, that horse you sold me is blind as a bat.'
The Chinaman says, 'I tell you he no lookee too good.'

SANDY   (loving it) You wouldn't believe it, wouldyer?

PRICKY   Who?

JOHNNO   (back at MICK) I'll pay you next week.

MICK   What're you going to do, row it out to me after they've flooded the place?

JOHNNO   What're you mean?

MICK   There won't be any next week here.

JOHNNO   Bloody hell.
   (then)
Then don't come the raw prawn about paying me next week.

MICK   I wasn't going to pay you next week.

JOHNNO   That's all right then. None of youse could row your way outa a paper bag.

SANDY   No need to get stroppy, Johnno.

JOHNNO   Tell 'em to keep out of it, Mick.

MICK   (to SANDY and PRICKY)   You heard me mate. No need to get down from yer high horses.

JOHNNO   (dutch courage)   LEAP OUT THE FIRST BASTARD!

   (No one moves)

MICK   (proof positive)   Weak as water.

JOHNNO   (sitting back down)   Not worth a man muddying his boots.

MICK (down at JOHNNO) That'll be another tenner you owe a bloke.

JOHNNO Come off it. What for?

MICK (winking at the others) For saving your good looks.

PRICKY For saving who's good looks?

MICK Come to think of \it, that'll be another tenner for saving on the ambulance you would have needed.

JOHNNO (rolling sleeves up) Right!

MICK (ditto) Right!

> *(They stride off to 'go around the side' to fight.*
>
> *SANDY and PRICKY watch them go with mild interest)*

PRICKY Who?

SANDY (answering) I'll lay you Johnno's tenner on Mick.

PRICKY I'll lay Mick's tenner on Johnno.

> *(SANDY notices POP stirring, and brings PRICKY's attention to it.)*

SANDY (whisper) Might be anotheee about Kidman.

POP (instead:) 'Late for Koorboora'? Gawd strike a light, I know how that saying got started, ya mugs. We were mining at Koorboora and we used to meet in the evenings. There was Dick, he was the 'mayor'. I was up in Otto's old place and Wilfred was in his own tin humpy, and every night we'd all congregate at one house, usually Dick's. As mining fields go, they all take turns to entertain at night.

Any rate, Dick was comparatively young then; he was only sixty-five or so. Wilfred the same and I was thirty. Wilfred would come down with his hurricane lantern about half past five or six o'clock and then we'd sit and talk till about eight.

Of course Dick would be up at four in the morning, coughing and smoking and drinking tea. You could hear him all over Koorboora. There was nothing left there, only bare stripped-out country, and these few old tin humpys.

So at about eight at night Dick would say in his cultured old school teacher's voice…. he would never insult anyone outright, he wouldn't'… he'd say, 'I'll just take a little look at the time'.

Of course we all knew what was coming. He'd go and make a great noise getting ready to kip down, throwing plates around and shifting billy cans, and of course we're all there waiting. Eventually he'd find the clock, 'Ah,' he'd shout out, and that was it. Out he'd come and say, 'You wouldn't believe: it's eight o'clock, boys! My word that's late for Koorboora!'

And that was the signal for everyone to leave.

    (has to pause in wonder)

Dunno why I started on about that…

SANDY 'Late for Koorboora', Pops.

POP What about it?

(But, anyway, there is a cry of pain and outrage off.

MICK comes back helping JOHNNO who is holding his head and dragging his feet. He helps him to his possie, puts a refresher bottle in his hand)

MICK (an explanation) Poor bugger only goes and trips over that bloody big rat. He steps back and bang over the bastard thing he goes and hits his head on the 'dozer. That's the trouble with driving a bloody bulldozer, them dirty rats following you everywhere. They can't leave 'dozers alone, those bloody rats can't. You can tell the real trouble makers in 'em too... they're the ones with pig tails.

PRICKY Who?

MICK (as though he asked) Not stuck on their heads, stuck on their bums.
    (then, thought)
Hey, anyone see bloody old Wally Jenkins in there pissing away in a corner?

JOHNNO (sitting up) His pay day today.

MICK He owes me a bob or two. No wonder he started shaking like a cur when he saw me coming.

JOHNNO He owes me too.

MICK Don't come that.

JOHNNO   He bit me last week

MICK   He bit me last month

JOHNNO   He bit me a year ago.

MICK   Bullshit!

> *(It looks like they are going to start up again. But PRICKY inadvertently comes in with the show-stopper:)*

PRICKY   Who?

SANDY   (adding to urgency)   Knowing Wally flamin' Jenkins, he could be in for that fifty. The way he can spread the bull, I'd be a bit worried… but then
   (meaningful at MICK and JOHNNO)
I wasn't in the hunt for that tenner like somes I know, either…

MICK   Sandy's right! That mongrel-on-the-sly Wally bloody Jenkins…!

> *(He and JOHNNO dash inside.)*

PRICKY   (all innocently)
Oh, the pretty girls of Bowen were handing out their duds.
I longed to have a chat with them so I made a beeline for their tubs,
When some curly children saw me and soon they raised my dander

Crying, 'Mother, quick, take in your duds; here comes the Overlander!'

(chorus)
So pass the billy round, boys, don't let the pint pot stand there
For tonight we'll drink the health of every Overlander.

> *(MICK comes haring back from around the left side of the building. JOHNNO comes haring back from around the right side of the building.*
>
> *MICK points him to go around the left side of the building, while he hares off around the right side of the building.*
>
> *They come back around to the verandah, panting but empty-handed.)*

MICK   Did a skinny looking redheaded bludger with pockets longer'n his arms choof around this way?

PRICKY   Who?

JOHNNO   Goes by the name of Wally or Stingy…

PRICKY   Who?

MICK   Bloody Wally bloody Jenkins, who else? Cripes, what's up with you?

SANDY   Oh, might you be talking about Wally Jenkins?

MICK Hand the dill over!

> *(SANDY and PRICKY point off in different directions.*
>
> *MICK takes off around the left side of the pub, while JOHNNO takes off around the right side of the pub.*
>
> *SANDY and PRICKY wait patiently for them to finally emerge together, but still empty-handed, from the front door.*
>
> *They are wiping fresh froth off their lips)*

SANDY (jealously) Where'd you get that?

JOHNNO (very coyly) Somebody's buying in there.

SANDY Why didn't you stay?

JOHNNO They weren't buying us.

PRICKY (hopefully) Any mention of us out here?

MICK Dunno. I'll go and see…

> *(He and JOHNNO goes back inside. They come back out a moment later, but with wiping more fresh froth off their chops again)*

MICK (mock apologies) Naw, you're better off out here. The flies are terrible in there.

SANDY (roused) I've a good mind to have a fling at that fifty.

PRICKY Who?

SANDY Me.

PRICKY (relieved) Thank Christ, I thought it'd gone.

SANDY That was the tenner. The tenner went off.

MICK There weren't no tenner, right?

PRICKY (irrespective of that) I was worried someone wouldn't get in with the one I heard not so long ago. Mind you, I wasn't there but all the others were there and they tell the tale. They went into the pub and Allan was across the bar, and now and then he'd stare at this Polish bloke. I don't think he'd ever seen this Polish fellow before, but this character was looking at him the wrong way or something.
Anyway Allen got drunker and drunker and said, "I'll belt this mug'.
All of a sudden he raced around to this bloke and he said, 'Come outside, I'll have you!', and he pulls out his tobacco and rolls a cigarette like going outside was the easiest thing in the world. He puts it in his face, lights it, and he blows smoke into the other fellow's face, going, 'Come on, come on'.
The Pole says, 'No need to go outside' and Allan said, 'All right, I'm a gentleman. I'll give you first hit. Come on, I'm a gentleman!'

Next thing 'BANG!', down went Allan, that cigarette splattered all over his silly looking moosh. The Polish fellow jumped on Allan and was bashing the living daylights out of him and the publican had to pull him off on the threat of no more beer.

As soon as Allan could get up he said to his mates, 'A great lot of mates, you lot are; wouldn't give a man a hand'.

SANDY Naw, that's not as good as when old Carl gets hit by that pig.
    (to PRICKY)
You tell me that one?

PRICKY Who?

SANDY Well, listen and learn something. There was this 'ere pig that was bailed up and broke away from the dogs and come straight down the ridge. It was wet weather and Carl slipped on a vine and the pig hit him and the tusk went into his arm and laid it open to the bone. Carl had to go into the hospital and he's waiting in the out-patients, you know how they make you wait and wait.

Finally Carl says, 'I've been sitting here and there's blokes coming in with little scabs on them and pimples, and women with warts and things like that, and one thing and another. They are treating them and treating them, and I'm sitting there, drip, drip, drip, a bit pool of blood. The bloody old dragon of a matron walking around there, been drinking vinegar all last night for sure; you could tell by the look on her face. Hour after hour I'm still sitting there and the pool of blood's getting bigger and bigger. At last a girl comes over to me with a book and she says, 'What's your name?'

'Thank buggery. Name's Carl Arn.'

'What's your father's name?'

'Otto Arn.'

'Mother's name?'

I told her.

'What's her mother's name?'

I told them the family history going back for five hundred years and signed a lot of papers and one thing and another and they asked me was I married and I said, 'Yeah, can't you see the look on my face?'

'Why did you marry? And what's her name? What's her father's name? What was her mother's name?'

She goes back through that side of the family for three hundred years and the pool of blood is getting bigger still and I'm getting weaker and weaker. In the end I just lost me bloody temper and I stood up and started waving my arm around splattering up their nice clean bloody floor and I bloody shouted, 'You mob of mongrels in here; isn't there a bloody doctor in the joint who cares what a real bastard of a wild pig is watching'n'thinking?'

That really got them going and in a few minutes they had five doctors running around giving me drinks of water and had me stitched up in no time.

Like I said, you've got to open your mouth at times or next time a pig comes at you what're you going to do? Nothing! Nothing's gonna stop it if it thinks all you've got is sitting there in your own pool of blood. It's not right to let pigs think they can play the merry hell like that.

MICK (suddenly pointing out) There he goes!

(JOHNNO leaps to his feet, goes to dash off, but MICK grabs him first)

MICK (calling sweetly) Hey, Wally...? Good to see you, Wal...

JOHNNO   Did you see that?!

MICK   Bloody hell! There's nothing to that Wally Jenkins, but I never seen a man jump over a bulldozer like that.

PRICKY   I ain't ever seen a rat chasing a man jump over the bulldozer, either.

SANDY   It mightn't been the rat.

PRICKY   It might've been a pig, after all.

SANDY   Naw, pigs can't fly over bulldozers like that.

PRICKY   What about a pig's arse with a lot of rat up front?

SANDY   Yeah, that'd be a different matter…
   (then)
Where were we?

   (Silence, before:)

POP   'Olympics'? Talking about the flamin' Olympics and long jumps, I was working on Strathmore Station and Stan Forwall the head stockman asked me if I could drive a truck. Well, I had driven an ordinary truck… kinda… but he asked me if I could drive a blitz wagon. I thought it'd be pretty similar, so I said yes.

Now there was this mob of young jackeroos just took on and a heap of pack saddles to be shifted out to the twelve-mile camp just over the twelve-mile creek. I thought I'd have a bit of fun with these wet-behind-the-ears jackos. They were all sitting around the blitz there scratching their heads over what they were looking at.

I walked around that thing two or three times looking like an expert, looking at the tyres and clicking my tongue and shaking my konk, and that sort of got them a bit more worried.

I said to one young fellah, 'You know what this is?'

'No.'

'You've never seen a blitzer before?'

'No.'

'Any o' youse?'

'No.'

'This's a motor car come lorry come truck come tractor, orright?'

'We still ain't ever seen one.'

Anyhow, after a bit of trouble I get the old bomb going. Stan told me she had no brakes and he said when I come to the twelve-mile creek to put her in reverse when I had to stop if I couldn't find any soft tree around there, like. So I loaded them young jackos and the saddles in the back and got started.

I couldn't find any reverse Stan was talking about but I thought what the buggery there's got to be soft trees around the twelve-mile camp since he mentioned it without being asked.

Off we go. We were going along the track and all the jackaroos started to sing a bit. I thought I'd show them getting so cocky and confident in me driving. So I ran over this big tree root, went in the air five or six feet and come down with a biggest thump you ever seen.

I heard a lot of yelling from the back and tried to pull up but there was no brakes, was there?, and I only managed to pull up four hundred yards down the track and I said, 'What's all the yelling about?'

'Willy fell out,' one of them said.

This young Willy had been bounced out all right and he'd taken two or three pack saddles with him. I said to him, 'What's wrong with you?'

'I fell out.'

'There must be something wrong with you falling out like that.'

'I dunno what happened.'

'Well,' I says, 'don't let it happen again.'

So we started off again and this time got to twelve-mile creek without him falling off. That creek really had steep banks back then, and I thought cripes, no brakes, now what? Then I had an idea and I shoved it into four-wheel-drive where you don't need gears, not in those days... you just stick it into four-wheel-drive and go into neutral. Anyway, while I was trying to do that we took off down the bank. We didn't quite break the sound barrier, but we must have come near to it. Bang! Crash! Bounce and bash! And then halfway up the other bank I hear all this yelling and then the blitzer stopped just before the top and started to roll back down. I looked through the back window and all I could see was that silly little Willy buggerlugs and a heap of pack saddles all in an untidy heap in the middle of the creek below me. I thought I was going to hit him because I had no way of stopping. I've never seen anyone scatter like it; that kid scooped up all the pack saddles and got out of the way, and the blitz just see-sawed back and forth, up one bank then the other, till finally she stopped in the middle of the creek. Was I mad and that young'un Willy was just the excuse I wanted!

I got out and shouted at him, 'What's wrong with you?'

'Dunno.'

'You're always falling out and making me stop to pick you up!'

'I dunno why. I just keep falling out.'

'You going for the Olympic long jump or some mad thing?'

'No, sir.'

'Well, there's nothing wrong with this truck and there's nothing wrong with my driving. Now get back up in there or I'll start driving as rough as bags and then you'll be really sorry!'

So that got all the new jackos going. They all climbed out and started pushing and got that old blitzer up that bank and they kept pushing her all the way into camp. When we got there, I shouted, 'Whoa up!' and they did.

And that's how I got to twelve-miles without having to resort to any soft trees.

> *(MICK and JOHNNO come back to join them. They are even more forlorn about things)*

JOHNNO Have to admit that Wally's got legs.

MICK Come pay days, he's grease lightning.

PRICKY Who?

JOHNNO (cunning) Old Shirl put you on a promise, did she?

MICK You had yours last week!

JOHNNO Easy on... Just thinking, once upon a time one of Shirl's promises used to be worth a few of the old folding matter.
    (even more sly)
What'd you reckon it'd be worth now?

MICK (catching on) Raffle it, you mean?

JOHNNO   Just sayin'. Knowing those dorks in there are from the city and ain't got any sense of taste or smell left.

MICK   Let's go!

(They take off inside again)

SANDY   That wasn't bad, Pop, that one about falling off trucks. Got me thinking about that family who had that little mining show and Joe the youngest was a lad about eighteen. He was on with a girl at the Glacier Restaurant in town, a few miles away and they used to go into the dance on Saturday nights.

Well, Joe had very sweaty feet, and water was scarce. One night he picked up the girl and she said, 'Oh, Joe, you smell badly. What is it?'

'Oh,' he said, 'me socks I suppose. I've got sweaty feet after a six mile walk and there's not much water to wash socks.'

'Well, Joe, go down to the store and buy a new pair,' she said.

So he went down and it was open and he came back again wearing these brand new socks, and after a while during the waltz she started to phew-whiff again and she said, 'Joe, what did you do with the old pair of socks?'

'I've got them in my pocket,' he said.

POP   (suddenly piping up) I took out me teeth and put them on the bedside table to give the cockroaches something to play with. In the morning I rolled over and had a look at the clock to see whether it was time to get up. But not having my glasses on I couldn't see it properly. Still half asleep I reached around and found my teeth and stuck them in, and then had another look at the clock. I still couldn't see the time.

'Shit,' I said to m'self 'I'm going blind.'

PRICKY   That's all right about you being robbed blind, Pop. What about me? I was just about to make a move on that fifty with the one about that time in the mines. A bloke coming in above where anyone might be working would sing out, "On top!' to let everyone below know he was there. If there was anyone below they were supposed to yell out, 'Below!' Well, that's what they were supposed to sing out, but what they really used to sing out was 'Arse'ole!'

One day this old chap was bring down a couple of lady visitors to look at the workings and when he got in he shouted out, 'On top!, and none of you blokes sing out 'Arse'ole!' cos I've got a couple of sheilas here with me.'

SANDY   Yeah, and it would've served them right if you had've told it, too, mate.

PRICKY   You just have to blink and they whip things out of sight these days, let alone a fifty. Ain't that…
   (MICK and JOHNNO return shaking their heads in disbelief)
…right, Mick?

SANDY   (about MICK) What's wrong with him?

JOHNNO   Shirl's gone and half the bar's gone missing too.

MICK   Life bloody stinks!

PRICKY   Who?

MICK   (thought) Hold on, she can only be in the cellar out back!

JOHNNO   How come?

MICK   It's the only place room enough for her to get 'em in a long enough queue…!

JOHNNO   The rotten hounds!

MICK   (war cry) Bastards, that's my betrothed back there!

(He charges off, followed by JOHNNO.

The bulldozer is heard started. Gears engaged. It shakes the earth as it is driven past, and then a crashing of the back part of the pub being dozed in)

SANDY   I guess you'd say that fifty's no longer up for grabs.

POP   (hearing it) Is it tomorrow already? Don't think I won't sue the bloody dogs onto 'em first! You can laugh, but we were up at Stratford pub one night and one of the blokes with us was that Peter, you remember him. We used to call him the man with the magic thumb. No one could see anything wrong with it but he used to be off work for weeks with it on the strength of a doctor's certificate about his thumb being crook. Lucky bastard.

We'd be talking about what a wild bloke old Tiger could be and a bit later in came the old possum himself. We could see Peter was a bit toey about him when he joined us, and so someone gave Tiger the drum to act up to his reputation for a bit of a lark.

He was a great old ham of course and he started in to rant and roar as if he was going to pull the place down at any minute. After a while Peter got a bit of dutch courage back after staying quiet ever since Tiger'd come in… and he started correcting somethingorother Tiger was saying.

Tiger shouted back at him, 'Don't you answer me back or I'll come around to your house and pull your nose!'

Peter thought he was fair dinkum and said, 'Come round to me place, mate, and see what's-what. I've got a savage dog. A Doberman, and one word from me and he'll tear your throat out!'

Well, a week or two later we were over at the Knob and Tiger remembered the incident and said, 'Let's go round and see this savage beast then.'

We found out where Peter's house was and drove around and when we go through the front gate this medium small hairy Heinz dog comes up wagging its tail. Peter opened the door to see who it was.

'Where's this savage Doberman who's going to tear my throat out at one word from you? ' Tiger shouted.

'That's it,' Peter said, 'At least it's part Doberman, and it's very savage.'

'Well, let's see you give the magic word,' shouted Tiger.

'Attack!,' cried Peter, and the dog wagged its tail.

'Kill!' shouted Peter and the dog jumped up and down in lick Tiger's face.

'The trouble is,' said Peter, 'I've forgotten the word, but if I can remember it, this dog will tear your throat out.'

SANDY   Bugger it! I forgot my one about the dogs.

PRICKY   Who?

SANDY   That German up at the Daintree. My old man went up there one time and though he'd never seen him, the moment the old chap came round the corner with his bandy legs… three wild pigs could have gone through them at one time; his legs were just like boomerangs… my Dad knew him.

My old man said, 'That's the bloke Jack's always talking about. We'll have a yarn with him.'

So we go over and this old boy's pushing this enormous wheelbarrow and on it he's got a jam tart.

Well, I've seen tarts that Auntie Alice used to make; they use to make them into sulky wheels, but this one was bigger. You've never seen a jam tart like this sticking out over the side of that barrow there. Gigantic it was.

He's got this old hat on and a bit of a straggly beard. My old man and he said g'day and Dad said he was up here campaigning for the council elections, and the old bloke with the barrow said, 'You're just the bastard I wanted to see.'

And he started in on what was giving him the shits about the district… I forget what it was and didn't care then at that age. All I know was as soon as he started talking, these thirteen or fourteen little dogs… little yappy things… you could choke them with one hand… well, as soon as he got up a storm talking to my old man, those bloody little dogs, they sort of divided and started running around in circles, sort of, yapping, yapping, and then they'd turn back and make a dash for that wheelbarrow of his making for that great big jam tart he had on it. But that old bloke never missed a breath or one word; he just kept on picking the little dogs off the tart and throwing them off, throwing them off, throwing them out and off… and they'd all be hitting the ground and licking the jam off their chops and then they'd come back.

How he could talk so loud and fast and still control his left and hand hands throwing these dogs out of that barrow, I don't know. But finally he stopped in the middle of a sentence saying he couldn't stand there all day yakking because he had to go before 'these bloody dogs of mine', he said, forced him to abandon the wheelbarrow and go for a cardboard box or something to put the jam tart in…. 'A man already had to go and take it out of the back of the ute and put it in this barrow because it's got so small'. And he said the shearer down at the shed he was taking it down to were a picky lot when it came to his jam tarts and they got real shirty if his dogs ate more than their fair share.

Gawd knows how big that jam tart was to start with, but as I said it was even bigger than Auntie Alice's sulky wheels even at that stage. I dunno how many of those yappy little bloody dogs he had.

> *(They sit in silence again.*
>
> *There is another bout of laughter from inside, which cause PRICKY to roll his jaundiced eye to peer through the window)*

SANDY That mean the fifty's still going, y'reckon?

> *(As if to answer, MICK and JONNO come back very dirty. They ascertain no beer left for them in the stash, and don't bother to sit)*

MICK You buggers don't care about a man's morning breath.

SANDY Shirl?

MICK (justified) She was just stringing them along.

SANDY Still going through with that raffle then?

MICK Shit, I forgot about that raffle!

(with renewed hope, he and JOHNNO dash back inside yet again)

SANDY (after them yet again) Try to get that fifty boosted to a 100 to make it worth a man trying...

(But there is immediately angry shouting from inside, followed by the unmistakable beginnings of a fight turning into a general brawl)

SANDY A 100 must've got their goat up. Pity. For a 100 I might come out with how I was once tootling along Wild Dog Creek. You heard it? Of course you ain't. Keeping the best for last. Anyway, I'd been talking to the old fossicker about bush ballads when I noticed three wallabies slowly hopping up the gully towards the main camp, moving on all four legs in the ungainly manner they adopt when feeding.

We were sitting outside the old man's hut; he had upended an old fruit box and I was sitting on an engine block. The wallabies showed no fear or even surprise at our presence. They only stood swaying slightly to have a good look at us, and then resumed their feeding. I expressed surprise at their tameness.

The old fossicker said, 'Well, you see, they all know me. When there's no one else around, they come up and talk to me.'

'You mean they grunt and that sort of thing?'

'No, no, they talk proper like, you know, just the same as the dog.'

(The fight inside is now going full swing.

SANDY picks up the last bottle. They take last swigs from it dolefully)

PRICKY   Last one.

SANDY   (philosophically) Tempus fugit.

PRICKY   Who?

SANDY   Last day too.   Almost forgot about that.

PRICKY   Real pity, that.

SANDY   Wasn't a bad old bastard of a place, when you think of it. Few years, you'n'me, Pop, here, eh? Got in a fair blighter of a rut under this bloody verandah, we did, I spose

    (MICK and JOHNNO re-emerge all bloodied)

SANDY   What happened?

JOHNNO   (scandalised)   Shirl only goes and puts the boot into him.

PRICKY   Who?

MICK   Bloody life stinks!

    (and huffs off. JOHNNO follows.

    In the hiatus that follows, SANDY holds up the last bottle; there is not even a drop left)

PRICKY Coming tomorrow?

SANDY Naw, couldn't stand to see even a coat of paint taken off the old place m'self.

PRICKY (sympathetic) Know what you mean..

> *(SANDY rises to leave. He is so 'wedded' to his spot over the years that when he gets up a piece of the verandah's floorboards comes away with him. He puts it back reverently and then walks off not realising a bit of it is still stuck to his backside.*
>
> *PRICKY shrugs his turn too, and:)*

PRICKY See you one day, Pop.

POP What?!

> *(When PRICKY rises, the old Fosters sign he has been leaning against all these years breaks up. He hesitates, looks down at it, shrugs, and leaves it fallen and busted there.*
>
> *POP seems to doze a moment in the evening light. Then he just carries on with:)*

POP A chap and I were going around looking for bloody propositions in West Australia gold fields. If you give a man a bob or two in those days you could take an option, and you and he sign that and it's legal. Now you've got his property for twelve months, and if you sell it he's on vendor's commission. Everybody's happy most times.

I might sell it for ten thousand quid. Tell a hell of a lot of lies, but the man I was with was prepared to do that. He was a new chum too. I lost a lot of money, but. I was a bloody mug of course. Anyway, this chap and I went to this town and we took a room. It wasn't part of the main house; it was set away a little. We put some biscuits and bread and other things in the room and went out. When we came back home there'd been a bloody cow in there and it had eaten all the bloody stuff and shit on the floor and went out.

I thought, 'What a bloody cow.'

Dunno if you know this, but the cow's got wonderful brains, and any new chum that comes there a cow like that bloody cow knows a new chum's breezed in and no matter where you come in the town it knows where you, the pushover, is at any given time, night or day. She knows you don't understand that and she comes and robs you and shits there just to let you know what a pushover you are.

Well, we went away from that dead-end town and come back in a couple of months, and we had all out food in the car – spuds, bread and biscuits. We stopped at the pub and when we came down next day that same bloody cow had been at the car, unlocked the doors and pulled the stuff out and done a lot of damage, including leaving her shitty calling card under the steering wheel.

She knew we were back! Wonderful brain, wonderful!

So I went to Thursday Island not long after. It was my first time there which made me a new chum, see, and I had a camp in the bush and there was a bloody cow come there knowing I was a new chum of a pushover and wouldn't know what's what with bloody cows!

But I did, didn't I?

I put some wire round the camp but that bloody cow still got through and ate everything and knocked everything over, and shit on the floor of course just to show me who's boss.

So I put a proper fence up, but the bloody cow got in again and does the same thing including the dirty doings on a man's floor.

I says to myself, 'I'll fix that bloody cow'.

I put the fence up again but this time I left a big gap so the bloody thing could come sailing on through… and I'd know where *it* was. So I hid in the camp willing to wait for as long as it took for that bloody cow to get in and think it's got the better of a bloke. This time that that bloody cow was going to get a two-by-four right between the eyes, right smack on that wonderful brain.

Well, I hid myself away and played possum until finally I see that bloody cow coming. So I braced myself.

I had a bit of fence post with a knob on the end like a club and I was going to do that bloody cow in or half do her in anyway. Didn't matter to me. I was sick of being shit on.

But, you mightn't believe this, that bloody cow went round the camp and she's pressing her head through the wire, not succeeding there, and moving on to another place and pressing her head through the wire again, not succeeding, then moving on to another place… going round and round that fence and everytime going past the big gap I left for her to sail on through. One time she's even got her arse-end inside the gap trying to get leverage to get her head through the wire from the outside.

So then she starts pressing her weight against the wire here and leaning against the wire there and still going round and round past the gap I'd left for her to sail on through. One time she tried to lean her weight where the gap was and nearly fell on through, but on she went to try another place. Talk about cunning. See what a wonderful brain that's no mug…?

Any rate I'm still waiting and hiding in there. I was thinking to myself just keep waiting her out and when she cottons on to the gap being there and she sails on through, boy, is she going to get it right on the noodle, wonderful brain or no wonderful brain.

But do you know that bloody cow kept sticking her head through those fence wires and leaning her weight against them and walking past the gap I'd left for her to sail on through, until she gave up and wandered off.

Clever, you wouldn't read about it.

And the thing was I never did get a go at that bloody cow.

(Fade to blackout)

www.ingramcontent.com/pod-product-compliance
Lightning Source LLC
LaVergne TN
LVHW051703080426
835511LV00017B/2711